101
COMMON MISTAKES
IN ETIQUETTE
-And How To Avoid Them

by
EMILY POST

NEW HAVEN, CONNECTICUT

A. D. STEINBACH & SONS, INC. 1939

PRINTED BY *A. D. Steinbach & Sons, Inc.,* NEW HAVEN, CONN., U. S. A.

ACKNOWLEDGMENT *is hereby made to my publishers, Messrs. Funk & Wagnalls Co., for their kind permission to use a certain few paragraphs from my books, "The Personality of a House" and "Etiquette, the Blue Book of Social Usage."*

—EMILY POST

CONTENTS

ILLUSTRATIONS

INTRODUCTION

At some time or another we all make mistakes — perhaps very slight, thoughtless ones, or perhaps those about which we ought to have known better, or perhaps again we are greatly disturbed by personal concerns, and for the moment callously unobserving. But none of us is proud of doing awkward things or of being thought tactless or inconsiderate by our neighbors — even though they are themselves too courteous to let us notice their criticism.

As a matter of fact, there is small excuse for any of us in not having learned the essential everyday rules of polite behavior so thoroughly that their observance has become automatic — such rules, for example, as smiling when we say, "How do you do!" and answering "Very well, thank you," no matter how far from well we may happen to feel. And yet, among these same essential rules there are many which — judging by repeated questions sent me — thousands find perplexing.

In this little book, therefore, will be found directions not only for the would-be successful hostess, but for every woman who would like to create an inviting atmosphere of "home," whether she lives in a house of important size or in the smallest bungalow or city apartment. Answers to these principal questions of the moment include: "Do you serve yourself first or last when you have women guests at your table?" "Do you think it is in good taste to wear 'bare-toed' sandals with an evening dress?" "Do you apologize for wearing gloves when shaking hands?" "Do *you* hesitate — wondering whether or not it's proper to remove your hat in a restaurant?" "Are you at a loss when you want to refuse a cocktail?" "Are you nervous at the thought of 'entertaining guests'?" "What should you do when visitors stay until your dinner hour, and you have not a thing in the house with which to make an extra dish?" "Do you know how to give your living room the quality of inviting charm?"

These questions and scores like them, I have answered in the pages that follow. I have purposely avoided putting them into "do's and don't" lists because I know very well that "tables" are not only uninteresting to read, but that their disconnected form makes them hard to remember. I have, therefore, included the answers in the general material. But the details given are many and practical, and it is my hope that they will be found useful in helping you to be a gracious hostess, and to enable you to make your home a livable, lovable center of charm in the community where you live.

CHAPTER I

THE RULES OF FORMALITY

Will following the rules of etiquette make you appear stiff, formal, and artificial?

Do the so-called "rules of formality" make life more difficult or make it run along more pleasantly — more smoothly?

Too often we think of formality as something stiff and constrained and self-conscious and artificial. Improperly applied it can be all of these and more, but properly applied it contributes to ease and dignity and beauty not only out in public among strangers but in our most intimate life at home. Almost every thing we've been taught to do that adds smoothness to the running of our houses, or pleasantness to family as well as neighborhood relationship, follows a precept of formality which has as its object a contribution to beauty. It may be beauty of form, or outline, or ease, or pleasantness, but it is beauty nevertheless.

For example: we say we set our dinner table formally; we mean neat regularity, because higgledy-piggledy scattering of plates and napkins, knives and forks and spoons is not as pleasing to the eye as a table properly (which is formally) laid. We rise to greet our guests! Again because the prescribed formalities of courtesy are pleasanter to the one arriving, than would be the sight of a family stretched out upon sofas or lolling in easy chairs not bothering to look up from their books or newspapers or whatever their occupations.

In other words, a child's earliest training in the formalities is not a party-dress trimming, it is a never lost advantage which throughout his life gives quality to the speech, the conduct, and the impulse of the thoroughbred.

In their general and impersonal applications, the purpose of formal (or ceremonial) rules is perhaps best illustrated by a church service. It would be shocking to have people trotting in and out of pews, talking out loud or otherwise disturbing the dignity associated with church ritual. For this reason, we have set rules of procedure for all ceremonial functions, so that marriages, christenings, funerals, as well as Sunday services, shall be conducted with dignity and smoothness. In short, every rule of etiquette to be worth following, must have for its object the smooth running of the social machinery, or the consideration of taste or of courtesy. Rules for social machinery include all details of dining room service, table manners, introductions, leaving cards, the unending details such as when to sit and when to stand, and the conventional (practically mechanical) thing to do and say on every occasion.

These random examples indicate the fact that knowledge of and practice in the formalities of courtesy, are essential to the beauty of living — essential to hospitality — essential to our most intimate lives.

CHAPTER II

The Personality of a House

I doubt if any subject can be nearer to the heart of every woman than that of creating an atmosphere of homelike friendliness in the house, the apartment, or the rooms that she and her husband call "home." So let us first of all consider those elusive qualities of homelikeness and inviting charm.

Does the personality of one's home depend solely on the amount of money you spend in furnishing it?

The personality of a house is not a mere question of outlay. Far from it! For instance, how many times when we are shown through a house of impressive value, do we keep thinking to ourselves, "Of course, all this is very splendid, but I wouldn't want it for myself — not a bit!" In fact, only on rarest occasions do we go into a house — or a room — that warms our hearts with its smiling beauty, its welcoming friendliness. Perhaps its furnishings are priceless; perhaps they have no value at all! The last is quite as likely as the first, since a house of appealing charm is possible at surprisingly moderate cost to almost any of us who CARE enough to *think* about what the beauty and comfort of home really means to *us*. And then assemble our furniture with intelligence and ordinary common-sense.

How should a home-maker choose furnishings? To make an impression on others? Or to make the room really livable?

In addition to such beauty as color and objects chosen solely for ornament, the first rule of common-sense for making a living room beautifully friendly, is to make it livable.

"LIVABLE" MEANS JUST THAT!

What's the best test to apply when buying a sofa?
In furnishing your living room, should the looks of the room or the habits of your family be the first consideration?

There should be at least one deep inviting sofa; at least one, or if possible two, deep comfortable chairs placed so that each is within reading distance of windows in the day time, and of perfectly adjusted and sufficiently bright lamps at night. Next to the easy chairs as well as at each end of the sofa, there must be a convenient table or stand upon which to put a cup and saucer or an ash tray or a book, or a work-bag or any other objects to use. It is necessary of course that there be a number of small chairs which can be drawn near the sofa or the big chairs for conversation, or placed around tables for bridge or other games. As a matter of fact, if the family is in the habit of playing constantly, a table always set for backgammon or cards is an appealing arrangement in a room big enough to make this arrangement incidental. In the same way a picture puzzle or any other evidence of interrupted occupation gives a lived-in effect.

WELCOMING FURNITURE

In arranging furniture, which should come first — looks or comfort?

It is true that the embellishment of beautiful detail of interior architecture or lovely pieces of furniture, and other possessions of value, or the friendliness of an open fire in winter, or the supreme beauty of a garden view in summer, are within reach of the comparatively few. But it should be remembered that *welcoming* arrangement of furniture costs not a penny more than an awkward arrangement that is never polite, and sometimes actually rude to the friends who come to see us.

What about placing your sofa in front of the fireplace with its back to the entrance of the room?

And yet, how often do we see a wing chair — intended for the coziest sort of comfort — parked off alone in a corner with neither window, lamp, table or companionable chairs, anywhere near. How many sofas are placed like unfriendly barricades straight in front of the fire-place, flanked moreover by two ponderously unmovable chairs, all three rudely turning their backs upon each entering visitor.

PLEASE ANALYZE THE WORD "LIVING"

Does it pay to buy a sofa or chair that ignores human anatomy just because it "suits the room"?
Should you choose lamps to look at or see by?

How many living-rooms offer nothing more restful to spend hour after hour in, than a sofa that is narrow and hard and bench-like, or short back-prodding chairs of modernistic design that utterly ignore the existence of human anatomy. As for lighting — how many are there who endure lights to look *at* rather than to see by? Lights either shining in our eyes or snuffing shades that throw the light-rays downward and reaching barely to our knees — impossible to read or to work by.

What's the main thing to consider in buying a desk?

A room that is completely, restfully, comfortable, can alone have the quality we call "homelike." It matters surprisingly little if old sofas or chairs commandeered from the family discards, be shabby or even ugly. If only they are restful to sit on or lie down upon, their ugliness can be made to vanish under embellishing slip-covers. It is true we would all prefer beautiful pieces of furniture, but if we can't have everything we want, it is consoling to remember that any object which is *suitable to use* has for this reason alone an inevitable appeal. For example, a broad-topped not at all beautiful work-table in the study of a writer, is far more appealing than the most perfect Eighteenth Century desk of miniature size. The first, stacked with notes and files and reference books, is obviously comfortable, and the second, for this same purpose would be just about as uncomfortable as a butter plate on which to eat one's dinner.

THE FIRST REQUIREMENT IS COMFORT

Comfort is the Cinderella of house-furnishing in contrast to the proud step-sisters "Cost" and "Display." It is not meant by this that objects of beauty are of little value! On the contrary! It is obvious that beautiful objects contribute to a beautiful room and yet cost as a standard of beauty could not be a less accurate test. But in considering beauty when applied to an object not purely decorative, its value should be measured first of all by its suitability to use. If in addition to this it be suitable to

A Living Room, Homelike and Comfortable

situation, it will have passed at least half of the requirements essential to homelike charm. Many simple little
houses that have scarcely an object of value are completely friendly, convenient, and delightful. Many great
houses are so austerely unwelcoming and so obviously
uncomfortable, it is a wonder that their owners can bear
to live in them.

AN ATMOSPHERE OF HOMELIKE CHARM

*Does one have to sacrifice comfort in order to have a
smartly furnished house?*

If you will bring to mind the inviting charm that certain people's houses always have no matter where they
happen to live, you will find that charm is of the sort that
gives to a mere "house" the appealing atmosphere of
"home;" that it is always an outward expression of in-
nate understanding of homelike habits of living. The
wrong approach to the problem of creating a room of
homelike charm, is to consider it as something to look at—
like a dress to wear at a ball. If we would draw a parallel
between the design for a dress, and design for a living
room, we should think of it in terms of English country
clothes; that is, in terms of usefulness, durability and comfort — which would be the diametrical opposite of at-
tention-attracting elegance (or eccentricity?) at no matter
what discomfort.

A PALACE OF DISCOMFORT

*Should you follow out some "period" in arranging your
house — or think first of convenience?*

In one of our warmer states, one replica of a Spanish
palace that I have in mind has a dining room across an

The Doorway Leads To We Know Not
What Charm Within

open court yard, so that if it rains the only entrance that
is indoors is through the servants' wing and kitchen. Every
floor is set with uneven tiles, all doorways on the entrance
floor are doorless, and every chair and sofa is narrow and
stiff and either of wood or of leather stretched as hard as
a drum. At night the candlelight is beautiful of course,
but to read by, not even a dozen candles make a happy substitute for the steady brightness of electric light — which
is not to be found in any of the company rooms — though
I believe it is admitted in the service end. By day, each
window has heavy bars of turned wood that make black
stripes across the sunlight, but not a fly screen in one of
them. And when those who stay in the house take a bath,
they walk varying lengths of corridors and flights of steps
to a bath building! This might very well have pleased the
people who lived four hundred years ago, but to most of
us who are living now, comfort presupposes screened protection from insects; bath rooms conveniently near bed-
rooms; floors that one can walk on without picking one's
way lest one's ankles turn; chairs and sofas that are restful
to sit upon and at night adequate light. Comfort also
means perfect adjustment to whatever it may please you
to have to do — in short, it means the adaptability of the
house that is yours, to your family, and to you.

THE HOUSE THAT SUITS YOU

*What's the best way to test the suitability of your
furnishings?*

The best way that I know to test the suitability of your
house is to study it exactly as a stage manager studies the
stage setting for each act of a play. In imagination put
each room through the ordinary tests that will be required
of it. From the point of view of a visitor, is the view of
it from the door of entrance attractive, or is it blockaded

by furniture that you have to walk around? Are you led
to a comfortable looking group of chairs, or is each chair
standing off by itself? Can three or four people talk easily
to each other?

*Should chairs be grouped together or placed separately?
What about placing chairs out of the way, close to the
walls of the room?*

Grouping chairs is always something of a problem,
since they must not be allowed to separate and stand
against the walls, nor must they gather as though for a
game of ring around the rosy. The question of *what* pieces
of furniture to get if you are a new house owner (or apartment tenant) is something that you yourself must decide.
But perhaps it may be useful to you if I describe my own
room. If you don't like it, you can cross every suggestion
off. I say "my room" because no matter where it is or what
style its furniture, it always has, and I'm sure it always
will follow, *precisely* the same pattern. Moreover, I always assemble it in exactly the same order. This then
is my personal list without which no room has any charm
for me.

MY OWN FURNITURE LIST

*What are the 3 main things to look for when buying a
sofa?
When is a sofa a "false pretender"?*

The first item is a completely comfortable sofa—meaning one that is low and deeply soft and with arms of just
the right height to rest my elbows when sitting in one of
its corners and against which to prop a cushion when lying
down. An armless sofa is to me the object of the most
irritating discomfort ever devised because it is a tantaliz-
ing reminder of the comfort it lacks. I'd far rather have a
wooden bench. It is at least not a false pretender.

How can you make sure of enough light for your sofa?
Will wall-bracket lights suffice as reading lamps?

First then, a pillow type of sofa drawn near enough to a window for light. Perhaps directly in a window — or in front of a row of windows. At each end of the sofa (if the sofa is flat against the window), a table and a lamp. Or else a long table the whole length of the sofa with lamps back of the end cushions. Then several chairs — two or three — big enough to be comfortable but not immovable and elephantine, and also a stool or two (seats, not footstools), near the sofa. Also small tables near at hand, with books and magazines for me; cigarettes and ash trays for friends. As to lighting — side brackets on the walls to be considered solely for becomingness to room and not considered as light to read by or sew by. Also there must be lots of books. In short, the requirement of a room of charm to me, is that it shall be completely satisfying to my personal habits of living. I don't play, and I don't like strumming, therefore, I *never* have a piano in my room. This of course may be your *first* requirement.

REQUIREMENTS FOR AN IDEAL HOUSE

How important is color in decorating a house?

Whether the house be big or little, ideally it must be snugly warm in cold weather, and well ventilated and cool in summer. It must have windows that create a proper draught when open and that won't rattle when closed. It must have shutters that won't bang, roofs that won't leak and it must have chimneys that draw. There must be a convenient and pleasant pantry and kitchen with all necessary appurtenances thereto and plenty — an overamount — of closet room. For me it is absolutely essential that there be beauty of color (if necessary applied by myself — with a paint brush — and however many yards of chintz). In addition to this, as much beauty in its furnishings as can be contrived. But the synonym of a homelike charm is the homely (homey) word: COMFORT.

SHALL WE HAVE A DINING ROOM?

Until a few years ago, the size of the dinner or the lunch a hostess might give was definitely limited to the number of places that could be laid on the dining room table and leave sufficient space for service behind the chairs of those seated. The dining room moreover, was considered not only essential to hospitality but indispensable to properly ordered family life. But at the present moment no question is more often asked me by those who are building or re-modeling a house, than this one:

How can one decide whether to have a big living room and no dining room — or a small living room so as to have a dining room?

"Shall we have a big living room and do without a dining room, or shall we have a small living room in order to give the dining table a whole room to itself?"

Need it be embarrassing to have company for meals when one has no dining room at all?

The answer to this, it seems to me, depends not merely upon the appearance of small rooms or big, but upon your own social habits and tastes. If you do not like crowds, a cosy little sitting room should be ample for your few guests; and if you are super-sensitive to neatness, you will probably prefer to keep your eating and living, as well as your cooking and sleeping hours, apart. In short, this same answer applies to the popular one-room apartment in which a very big room with its pull down beds and its behind-the-doors kitchen, serves all the purposes of four rooms. If you love crowds, and if you love informality, then the size of one huge general room would compensate not only for the lack of a separate dining room, but even for a kitchen and a bed room!

But to continue the dining room in the living room question: If your furnishings are to be modernistic then you would probably prefer a big living room and dining room combined, especially if your floor is laid with lino- leum, and your rugs, let us say, do not encroach upon the dining table end. On the other hand, if your furnishings are Georgian and your floor is laid with a carpet or with a thick rug, then a table constantly walked around, in ad- dition to the risk of spot-making crumbs falling upon the carpet, might make you decide on two rooms.

What's the important thing in choosing dining room chairs?
What should you do to determine the correct height of the dining room table you choose?

A very important point to suggest is that whatever fur- nishings you decide on, you must be sure that they fulfill their purpose of suitability to *you*, by putting whatever you intend to buy into practice as well as you can. Although a dining room chair is not chosen for its restful ease, an un- comfortable back that hits you at the waist line, or a heavy one that is difficult to move becomes increasingly annoy- ing with daily use. It is important to sit in the chair and draw up to the table. You may find that the frame of the table comes down too low for the height of the chair so that you can barely get your knees under; or you may find the chair so low that the table comes almost up to your shoulder.

Murals Make This Dining Room Spacious

CHAPTER III

The Most Important Table Appointment Is Silver

What is the danger in choosing silver of an ornate pattern?
What are the disadvantages of choosing plain silver?

Every bride, or for that matter, every woman who is moving into a new house or apartment and is therefore interested in the setting of her table, should remember when selecting her silver that she must like it — not just at first sight but for always. Many patterns which please at first sight develop annoying details. Certain patterns are hard to keep clean. Others are uncomfortable to use. And discomfort has a way of increasing. Some lovely-to-look-at crystal handled dessert forks and spoons of my own are so heavy in the handle compared with the bowl that people often drop them. A set of knives that I know of hurt everyone's palm. Implements too big or too small are equally uncomfortable. The point is that while you are choosing, pay attention to questions of upkeep and comfort. Remember too that perfectly plain silver (my own preference) shows scratches and requires a more brilliant polish than that which has some ornamentation.

MARKING YOUR SILVER

*Should a bride have her silver marked with her own
or her future initials?*

Which is preferable — plain or ornate lettering for silver?

This is of course a question of your own taste. The only
advice I would give is to avoid anything that can be called
novel lettering. For the reason that it is to be in use for a
lifetime, silver marking should be severely conservative.
A bride's silver is marked with her own or her future
initials, whichever she prefers. Either is correct.

The number of spoons, knives and forks that you must
have depends upon the number of people you are likely
to seat at your table, and upon the number of courses you
serve. If you intend to give dinners for twelve or more,
you must have twelve or more of each variety of implement you are to use. If there are never to be more than
eight or perhaps six at table, then your maximum requirement is eight or six implements for each course you serve.

In the following list the dinner service is for eight.

A COMPLETE LIST OF FLAT SILVER

12 tablespoons. (Eight for soup in plates, four for
serving spoons.)

16 or 24 small forks. (In best appointed houses small
forks are exactly alike whether used for fish, entree, salad,
dessert, or breakfast. If you can have unlimited dozens,
fish knives and forks are proper — if you like them —
but other special forks for special foods are unnecessary.)

16 silver-bladed knives. (Or subtract 8 and add 8 fish
knives — 8 for fish and 8 for salad. If you have the
American prejudice against the salad knife, then get only
8 knives for fish, and avoid serving items that require a
knife such as hearts of lettuce, unrestrained greens,
Camembert cheese, etc.)

12 large forks. (Called dinner forks; 8 for the meat course and 4 for serving forks.)

8 large sharp steel-bladed dinner knives. (For meat.)

8 dessert spoons. (16 if you serve soup in wide bouillon cups or Chinese bowls.)

8 after-dinner coffee spoons.

To this dinner list must be added these lunch and breakfast items:

8 teaspoons. (To be used for tea or coffee in a breakfast cup — or for bouillon at luncheon, if your bouillon cups are small.)

8 butter knives. (Never called "butter spreaders" outside of a silver manufacturer's catalogue.)

To this list add only, if you need:

8 ice-tea spoons. (For iced coffee or tea if you serve it.)

8 oyster forks. (If you serve oysters or clams or shellfish cocktail.)

8 fruit knives and forks. (If you serve whole fruit.)

To the above list you of course add pieces if you are giving dinners of ten or twelve. Or add extra forks and teaspoons, let us say, if you give big buffet parties. Or perhaps add special implements such as nut crackers and nut-picks, or lobster claw-picks, corn-on-cob handles, silver skewers, grape scissors, pepper grinders, etc. But the knives, forks, and spoons listed are *complete* according to best standards of taste for the setting of both formal and informal tables. Obviously, of course, you subtract whatever you are not going to need — or must do without for the time being.

AVOID UNNECESSARY SPECIALTIES

How can you avoid the danger of cluttering your silver chest with pieces you'll never use?

*Does setting the table with too many types of forks, etc.,
show poor taste?*

Even though some manufacturers will perhaps protest,
I must advise against cluttering your silver chest with unnecessary implements merely because they are listed in a
catalogue as intended for this or that item of food. As a
matter of fact, I can't see that it makes any difference to
the manufacturer whether you buy 24 plain small forks
that are alike — and correct according to best precepts —
or whether you buy 8 plain, 8 fancy, and 8 of another fancy
variety. If you choose no matter what, because you *like* it,
that is quite all right! But to think you must set your table
with an especially designed fish fork and another especially
designed salad fork and another especially designed entree
or ice-cream or for-anything-else fork is not only impractical but not even in good taste.

In houses of greatest distinction, a conventional big
fork is used only for the meat course — for lunch as well
as for dinner. And the identical conventional small fork is
used for breakfast, as well as for every course (except
meat) at a lunch party or a dinner.

The additional items necessary for the service of dinner
or any other meals are pepper-pots and salt-cellars — a
pair between each two places — and a small round serving tray for each servant who waits at table.

*Is a complete silver service necessary or can one use glass,
china or chromium pieces to take the place of silver?*

Centerpiece, candlesticks (or candelabra), candy dishes,
platters and vegetable dishes, afternoon tea service and
tea tray, and after dinner coffee service and tray are additional items; indispensable to the complete equipment
of a house. But in the present day, even in elaborately appointed houses, glass or china, chromium, or painted tin
may equally well take the place of silver.

CHAPTER IV

A Test of Quality Is Linen of Quality

What determines the quality of linen damask — texture of the linen or embroidery and lace trimmings?

Just as the test of a practiced hostess is in dinner giving, the test of the formal dinner table equipment is the quality of its linen damask.

Linen that is beautiful because of its texture is something that the unknowing seldom if ever appreciate.

The hostess without tradition is apt to think if her tablecloths and napkins are thickly embroidered and heavily lace-trimmed, they are something to be proud of. Perhaps they are. Perhaps again they are not. It is true that lunch cloths, supper cloths and tea cloths, runners, mats and doilies can be trimmed as much as purse can pay for. A hampering qualification this last, since it must be pointed out that the more elaborate the trimming the greater necessity for fine quality. In other words, trimming must always be in addition to quality and not an attempted camouflage of its lack.

Beautiful damask is always heavily soft, and it has almost a satin sheen — but heavier, softer, finer.

A damask cloth is necessary however, only for a formally appointed dinner table as opposed to a lunch or supper table.

THE WAY WE RECOGNIZE A DINNER TABLE

What are the 3 details by which you recognize that the meal served should be called "dinner"?

The three details whereby dinner is definitely announced are:

(1)   A damask cloth.
(2)   Soup served in soup plates with *rims*.
(3)   Soup spoons of tablespoon size.

In present day fashion we call our evening meal dinner or supper, and our mid-day one dinner or lunch, and it may not matter that the table on which and the appointments with which we eat the meal we call dinner, is not dinner at all!

WHEN DINNER IS MORE ACCURATELY SUPPER

Does the evening meal have to be dinner when you have guests?

In my own house, except on the rare occasions when I really give a dinner party, my two meals, correctly speaking, are lunch and in the evening a hybrid mixture that would be dinner were a cloth laid, and soup in plates the first course! If I am actually inviting people to dinner — meaning a "dinner party," then white damask covers the tables, and soup is in rimmed plates and bread and butter plates are banned. Otherwise, the evening meal in my house called dinner from force of habit, should be called supper because the table is set without a cloth, soup is often in cups and bread and butter plates are always included. It sounds absurd, I know. But that is how it is. A table-cloth and rimmed soup plates announce dinner, just as a man's cutaway coat and top hat announce formal dress. Nothing can change this fact. Nor the other, that wearing a sack coat and derby is not wearing formal clothes.

Can you call a meal dinner if the table is not covered with a damask table cloth?

The white linen damask cloth is part of our Anglo-Saxon tradition of dinner ceremonial that had its beginning at the end of the uncouth period of eating on bare boards. Which is the wherefore perhaps that bare boards even though bridged and islanded with runners or squares or circles do not connote the dignity of linen damask. One cannot picture an uncouth company around a linen damask tablecloth of beautiful quality. One pictures instinctively ladies and gentlemen whose manners match these titles.

HEMMING TABLECLOTHS AND NAPKINS

Since several hundred brides a year ask about the marking and hemming of linen, I think it will be of practical use to the brides who read this book if I include these details here:

Should damask be hemmed or hem-stitched?

Damask should be hemmed, not hem-stitched. The tablecloth hem is about three-eighths of an inch wide — hemmed by *hand* of course. The best hem on a napkin is only an eighth of an inch and very finely sewn. The edges of very small napkins, such as cocktail napkins, are usually rolled. All napery is over-cast along the folded hem.

MARKING TABLECLOTHS AND NAPKINS

It is essential to complete beauty that fine table linen be embroidered with monogram or initials. On napkins a single initial is enough, but on larger articles an initial designed with a few additional lines to give the effect of a monogram is more effective and the expense is less than two initials.

Where should the initials be placed on a large damask table cloth?

Large damask tablecloths are marked on either side of center, mid-way between table center and edge of table.

On small damask cloths?

Small yard-and-a-half square damask tablecloths—ideal for meals served on bridge tables — are marked at one corner — about one third from the corner edge of the table (not the cloth) and two thirds from mid-center of the cloth — put either parallel with table edge or cross-cornered. Square monograms look well set in line with the table edges; irregular ones look best cross-cornered.

On napkins?

Very large damask napkins are marked in center, others are marked in one corner — cross-cornered usually, but sometimes straight. To decide about place for marking on napkins, the simplest way is to fold the napkin as it is to be folded for use, and then make a light pencil outline in the center of the folded space.

FOLDING LARGE NAPKINS

When the marking has been put in the center of a linen napkin, it is folded by turning it over on the wrong side and folding it into three parts; and then by turning the sides back, making a square. When the napkin is turned over right side up, the monogram is in the center of a smooth-edged square. If the square is not too big it is laid flat on the plate in a diagonal. But if it is very big, then it is folded so that the folded square is a rectangle — wider than high. And each side is turned under but not creased flat, making a soft roll. This is laid vertically on the service plate. Marking is cross-cornered in the first case, and straight in the second.

FOLDING SMALLER NAPKINS

Is it wise to fold napkins in fancy patterns?

Napkins that are 20 inches are marked across the corner and folded in nine. If left flat, these are laid diagonally on the plate; if rolled (making the marking more conspicuous), they are laid perpendicularly on the plate.

A smaller napkin is folded in four, with monogram toward lower edge of plate; then bend about one third of the top corner forward in a sharp crease, the point of this crease coming just above the monogram. Now roll under (do not sharply crease) the two side corners. You get a soft roll on your plate with the top looking like a turned down pointed collar, the bottom of it of course left as it was, and the two sides rolled under.

Another way of folding a small napkin, especially if it is impractical to put the napkin on the service plate, is to fold it in four and then fold it perpendicularly in half again, like a tall narrow book.

These are about the only foldings used. Fancy foldings have gone out of fashion.

CHAPTER V

CHINA

And now to continue our table appointments. As I have already said, china and glass are both at the moment in highest fashion — and by many hostesses preferred to silver. Each of course has its own advantage and disadvantage. Silver requires unending polishing. China and glass on the other hand, are easily broken. The disadvantage of china not all of one pattern, is that it does not look well mixed.

Can you use both china and glass dishes, mixed, for dinner service?

An all-glass decoration of the table, on the other hand, is particularly pretty and cool-looking in the evening in summer. Lovely tall candelabra with dangling prisms and the lights from the candles reflected in the glass, display a table at its best. I like white better than colored glass, but this is purely a personal choice. For that matter, there is no reason why glass and china may not together decorate a table. In fact, the one handicap of china decoration on a dinner table, is that china candelabra are almost impossible to find, and china candlesticks are either flat on the table (which I dislike) or else they suggest bed-room mantel ornaments rather than dinner table decoration. Glass candelabra with china centerpiece and dishes are doubly lovely.

In my opinion, the loveliest table I myself ever set was all of glass with a Lowestoft flower-bowl, candy dishes and plates. My first choice is Lowestoft because in a Lowestoft bowl flowers are at their best. Why Lowestoft is so becoming I don't know, but it has an extraordinary faculty of blending itself with whatever flowers are in its keeping. It doesn't make any difference whether they are big flowers like peonies, gladioli or dahlias, or fragile ones like columbine; all the flowers in the garden are at their loveliest in such a container.

EXACTIONS OF CHINA

Can different sets of china be used together?

Its one exaction is that it be in harmony. Meaning that it have some matching detail — such as texture or at least a repeated note of color. In other words, service plates of one variety, bread and butter plates of another variety, centerpiece of another, dishes for sweets or foods of another, candlesticks of still another, would look like an odd-lot table at a rummage sale, unless these pieces were closely allied.

Whether you choose decorated china or that which is plain, is entirely a matter of your own choice. All white china of the same color and texture need not match in pattern or shape, but it would be unpleasing, for example, to use translucent milk china (actually glass) with opaque white earthenware. The attractiveness of china or any other plain color would necessarily depend upon the color of the cloth or table upon which it is to be set.

IF YOU CHOOSE A MIRROR PLAQUE

The question of whether a mirror plaque under your china centerpiece may be put on a table cloth, as well as upon a bare table, is something which your own taste must decide. The glass edge coming next to the linen never seems to me quite right. In the old table settings that had mirrored centerpieces, there was always a railing of silver or gilt surrounding the platform into which the mirror was set, and separating it from the cloth. The plain flat mirror of today laid upon a wood table, more particularly upon a table with a glass top, is very suitable. But this also is a question of your own liking.

Also, exactly like the list of flat silver which you must make to fit your personal requirements, the amount of china you buy is determined by personal need.

THE SERVICE PLATE

Is there a difference between the meaning of the words "service plate" and "place plate"?
Is the service plate a special plate used only for that purpose?

Just why, I don't know, but no questions about table setting are so often asked me as those about the service plate.

First then: Service plate and place plate are two names for the same plate.

Second: The service plate (or place plate) is not any specially set-aside plate different from any other plate. It is absolutely nothing more than the plate with which you choose — or happen — to set each place at table. According to the formal pattern of table setting, a plate is always put at each place instead of leaving an empty square of table cloth or table.

Should the service plate be larger, more ornate, than any other plate?

As to choice of service plate, the rule of good taste is this: If the service plate is larger, more ornate, and more conspicuous than all the other plates that are to appear in turn upon your table, it is plainly in bad taste. Properly, therefore, when setting your table you choose things that look well together. If you have a set of plates that harmonize with the flowers to be used in your center-piece you would naturally choose these plates for this particular meal. At another time you would set your table with plates that go with another decoration. In short, the only thing to remember is that service plates must be considered as part of the effect of your table setting as a whole.

What do large, dark-colored plates suggest? Pretty, small ones?

The other plates are noticed singly and in greater detail. Therefore, you naturally set the places at table with whichever plates best help the general effect, and then choose plates for your other courses that are most suitable for the particular foods to be served. Plates that are light in color and especially worth looking at, are usually selected for salad or dessert, because salad and desserts are rather prettier — and therefore, more becoming to fragile porcelain than either fish or meat. Large dark plates suggest meat; but white ones are equally suitable, except they ought not to be too fragile in type.

MEASURE YOUR PLATES

Sizes are important in that they ought not be either so little as to look like saucers, or so large as to look like plat-

ters. Meat plates should be larger than the other plates—
except those for broiled lobster, or for fowl and salad
eaten on the same plate. These both should be so especially large as never to be used for anything else. Otherwise, it is most important to choose plates that are in scale
with all of your other table appointments, especially with
the size of your flat silver.

Therefore, if your biggest forks measure no more than
$6\frac{1}{2}$ inches in length and if your soup spoons are scarcely
larger than dessert spoons and your dining room is called
a breakfast room and your dinner table top is three feet
square, then the largest plate that you could very well
use would be 9 or at most $9\frac{1}{2}$ inches for a dinner plate,
and 8 to $8\frac{1}{2}$ inches for the other courses. On the other
hand, if your dining room and its furniture is on a larger
scale and your spoons and forks and knives are, let us say—
big forks $8\frac{3}{4}$ to 9 inches long; small forks 7 to $7\frac{1}{2}$
inches; big knives 9 inches; small knives $7\frac{3}{4}$ to 8 inches,
then a dinner plate and possibly a service plate $10\frac{1}{2}$
inches would be proper.

SERVICE PLATES MUST NOT DISAGREE WITH
BREAD AND BUTTER PLATES

It is never quite possible to make your lunch table look
perfect when service plates and bread and butter plates
are not in harmony with each other. That they do not
match the plates which follow is much less important. But
even so, if you have not yet bought your china but are in-
tending to use different plates for each course, let me suggest that you get bread and butter plates of silver, if you
can (plated ones, if of good design, can be as good looking as sterling) or else get them to match your glass. On
the other hand, if you are choosing a whole set of matching china then there are no mixing questions of any sort.

You would, for example, set the places at table either with
your dinner plates, or with those of the next size smaller—
depending upon the scale of your table setting as a whole.

READY-MADE SETS OR PIECE BY PIECE?

*What's the first big question in buying a ready-made set
of china?*

*Is the number of pieces, or the number of pieces useful to
you, the all-important thing to consider when buying a
set of china?*

The question of whether to buy a ready-made set of
china, or whether to buy what you want piece by piece
from open stock, can only be answered by making a list
of the items you want and seeing whether the pieces in
the set will supply all of those in your list. Also (and of
most importance) compare the cost of all of the useful —
to *you* — pieces in the set, with the cost of these same
pieces bought separately out of open stock. If you happen
to find a set of attractive china at unusually small cost, it
might be wise to get it for use now, and later on collect better china piece by piece. But *don't* buy a set because its
cost adds up to a temptingly small amount, counted by
total number of pieces, instead of by those pieces which
you are going to use. Moreover, be sure that china which
you intend to use permanently, is of an established pattern that is reasonably certain to be kept in stock for years
to come. Remember that made-up sets which cannot be
matched are not economical, but extravagant since handles
off of cups, and chipped edges of plates, ultimately leave
you with broken-down equipment that you can never
repair.

HOW MUCH CHINA, AND FOR WHAT?

Beginning with breakfast: Instead of silver, perhaps
you choose a tea and coffee service of china. At all events

ordinary breakfast plates are about eight to nine inches in diameter. These same plates will be used for all courses at lunch or supper (eggs, meat, salad, dessert) and for all but the meat course at dinners. Your breakfast cups and saucers, if not too large, may be used for afternoon tea. The saucers for cereal at breakfast will do for soup, until you are able to add either dinner soup plates with rims, or cream soup cups and saucers for luncheons or informal evening meals. Cream soup cups seem essential in this day of informality, and in many houses the formal dinner soup plate from which soup is eaten with a table-spoon, makes its appearance not more than two or three times a year — if that!

The meat plate, as I have already said, is larger than the others, but every other plate used is from $8\frac{1}{2}$ to $9\frac{1}{2}$ inches and may be used indiscriminately for which-ever course at lunch, dinner or supper you think it best suited to.

One last word!

CHOOSE THE CHINA THAT DELIGHTS *YOU*

And that *you* think looks lovely in *your* room! That is best advice. If you go beyond this point, you can make up your mind to spend the rest of your life studying this lovely but difficult and unending subject. In any case, I strongly advise that you *do* go to the museum, if you live near one, or else spend hours at the library reading about, and looking at, the illustrations of china and silver and furniture, too. Because through learning to appreciate ex-cellence is the ONLY way whereby we can any of us develop our own knowledge and in turn, learn to exer-cise our judgment.

CHAPTER VI

The Strict Meaning of Formal Dinner

Is a big dinner necessarily a formal dinner?

Before describing any definite details of table-setting or party-giving, I must explain what I mean by the word "formal," because otherwise I will be thinking of one kind of party and you may be thinking of another, and we won't understand each other!

Strictly speaking, the word "formal" means ceremonial. A formal dinner is the most ceremonious social function that exists; I might say that *still* exists, since they are seldom given by hostesses younger than fifty! The younger fashionables of today give big dinners, but they almost never give formal ones.

Is it ever permissible for your husband to wear a tuxedo coat at a formal dinner?
Who serves a formal dinner?
Do average people have to give formal dinners?

Let me outline a formal dinner: A large group of ladies wearing their most elaborate evening dresses, their best jewels, and of gentlemen in tail coats. (The informal tuxedo coat won't do at all at a formal dinner.) Everyone is standing, because the hostess must stand at the door receiving. She greets each arriving guest with the same handshake, the same smile, the same phrase "How do you do?" To wave hand above head as a "Hello" to Mary at a formal dinner would be unthinkable. When dinner is announced, the host offers his arm to the lady of honor and leads the way to the dining room. The other gentlemen offer their arms — each to the lady assigned to him by the hostess — and follow two by two. The table setting is strictly formal and therefore may not include bread and butter plates, nor smoking equipment, nor food of any kind except ornamental fruits or sweets and salted nuts. Napkins must be on the service plates; moreover, proper service exacts that a truly formal dinner be served by a butler and footmen — or by caterer's waiters. If one should have women to wait at table instead of men-servants, the dinner would no longer be strictly formal. I think this is enough to indicate the picture, and if you want to know every detail of such a dinner, it is all in my enormous book "Etiquette," at the nearest public library. And if you are the wife of a Government official you will be obliged to give, as well as to go to, formal dinners constantly. But the advantage to most of us who are merely private citizens living in our own homes is that we don't have to give formal dinners. But can give dinners (as well as lunches and suppers) that are as informal as we please.

THE MEANING OF INFORMAL

Can a dinner be large and still informal?

But don't misunderstand the word "informal." Which doesn't mean "any old way" but means free from fixed rules of ceremony. Informal dinners can include a hundred guests, as well as they can be limited to four; they can be as lavish or as simple as you choose, and certainly they can be perfect ones — delightful ones — to which strangers quite as well as family or friends may be invited.

So let's forget all about this word "formal" — meaning ceremonial — and all its exactions, and consider the question of giving dinners as hospitably and as charmingly as can be.

And now let's begin with your dinner. The first thing to do, of course, is to decide upon the people you are going to invite. If you are giving that dinner of today's fashion, the big dinner at little tables, it does not matter so much about the people asked together, as it does if you are having very few for dinner.

THE GREATEST TALENT A HOSTESS CAN HAVE

What is the greatest talent a hostess can have?

Remember that an outstanding talent of the perfect hostess is the ability to bring people who amuse or interest each other. This means taking the trouble to think. For instance, a hostess who invites a real musician, with a piano strummer — who won't stop strumming, or invites a man whose only interest is sport, with a group which delights in metaphysics, is not taking the trouble to think.

Choosing people for a dinner is not usually as extreme as this, because you are rather apt to ask members of this group or that group together. The fact that there are groups in each community means that this group is amused by or interested in those things. Happily too, many of us know certain ideal guests who by their own tact and good temper fit in with every group and help to make a party go. When people sit in silence, it is invariably the fault of the hostess who has tried to combine a wrong mixture of people. If you are inviting people who belong in one group of intimates, it is simple enough. But if your guests are strangers to each other they should be selected with care.

CHAPTER VII

How to Give a Dinner

What are the 3 first steps in giving a dinner?

The first thing to do, of course, is to decide upon the number of people you are going to invite. Second, make your list of who they are to be. Third, send your invitations. If you are giving a formal dinner (meaning a dinner of ceremony) you should write notes in the third person. But, as I have said, since practically no one outside of diplomatic or official circles gives dinners of ceremony, let us say you telephone your invitations instead.

When the acceptances have completed your number, there is nothing to do further until it is time to select the menu. If your guests are intimate friends, the preference of those who are epicures or the allergies of one or two others will perhaps decide for you. Or, if so far as you know, your guests are neither over-critical nor otherwise difficult, then decide on whichever dishes your cook (or you yourself) can make especially well.

What is the best menu to choose when having dinner guests you are eager to please?

In any case, remember that the first rule, if you would be a perfect hostess, is to choose dishes — for no matter what type of meal — that you know will be good of their kind. It is far better to give your guests scrambled eggs, or stew, or baked beans — any dish that is perfectly prepared — than it is to provide a pretentious menu that is indifferently well done. But now, let us consider the definite details of the formal dinner table.

COMPLETE FORMAL TABLE EQUIPMENT

The items of a completely equipped formal dinner table are twelve:

1. A tablecloth, or whatever is to be the foundation of the setting.

2. A centerpiece, of fruit or flowers, or an ornament complete in itself.

3. A place plate (service plate) for each person to be seated at table.

4. Four candlesticks, or two candelabra, or all six.

5. Two or four dishes of sweets.

6. Flat silver — correct implements at each place for each course.

7. Glasses.

8. Salts and peppers (a pair between each two places).

*

9. Napkins.

10. Dishes for salted nuts.

11. Place cards.

* *Bread and butter plates are only for informal dinner.*

Correct Formal Dinner Table Setting

Mrs. Post's Own Table

SETTING THE TABLE

The setting of a formal dinner table begins with the laying of the felt; and upon this the damask cloth. Plain white damask is the most formal table covering known. It is laid with the sharp center fold running in a ridge and forming an absolutely straight line from the center of the head of the table (the wife's place) to the center of the foot (the husband's place). A lace and handkerchief linen cloth should be pressed smoothly and not show ironing folds. Or, if (for a lunch party) the center of the table is to be covered with a centerpiece or runner and mats, no fold should show.

Having laid the cloth, you next put a service plate at each place — and at equal distances from each other. If there is an up and down to the pattern, be sure that each plate is set top rim up! Its lower rim comes down about to the edge of the table.

THE CENTERPIECE

For the center of the table, flowers are loveliest in whatever you choose to put them; only remember that a very high arrangement is to be avoided at a table set for ten or less since it prevents general conversation by keeping people on one side of the table from seeing those on the other side. In the place of flowers, your center ornament can equally well be of silver, china, or glass, but it must be complete in itself; an empty bowl or vase won't do unless the bowl has a cover or the vase be an urn with a top.

THE CANDLES

The next objects to be put on are four candlesticks, or better, two candelabra — high ones are greatly to be preferred since they give dignity as well as lift the candle flames above the eyes. If you use low ones, then *please* put the thinnest possible white or cream shades over the flames. Whether you use candlesticks or candelabra, they go in equally balanced spaces at either end of the center-piece. If your table is very large and you use both, then, whether it is best to place the candelabra close to the cen-terpiece and the candlesticks out on the corners of the table or place the candelabra beyond the candlesticks depends upon which looks best.

Candles belong on every evening table, whether in win-ter dark or summer daylight, but have no place on a day-time table unless they are actually needed to see to eat by. In other words, they are correct on a still sun-lighted sup-per table but incorrect on a lunch table.

Four dishes of sweets are placed between the candle-sticks and the centerpiece, or two dishes are placed in front of the centerpiece on the sides or the ends, wherever there is most room.

All objects on the table are as evenly balanced as pos-sible.

NEXT, THE FLAT SILVER AT THE PLACES

The amount of flat silver to be put beside each plate de-pends upon the menu to be served and depends also upon the service — since rules must be modified according to expedience.

In a formal house with many servants, three forks and two knives are the most allowed for the table setting.

In Victorian days when fashionable dinners included nine or ten courses, it was impossible to find place for (or to supply all at once) such armies of silver. It became the rule, therefore, that no more than three forks should be put at the left of each plate, and four implements at the right side. When practical, these numbers are still adhered to, but if there are no servants to make this bringing on of extra forks and knives easy, it is merest common sense to put all of the implements to be used on the table when it is set, or to make whatever other change of rule may seem expedient.

For example, the question of which fork to choose is no problem if the table be properly set, since the outside implement is always the one you are meant to use. In setting the table, therefore, you put the fork, or knife, that is to be used last, next to the plate, and mentally continue the courses backward until the implements for the first course are on the outside (farthest from the plate).

SALAD FORK FIRST

Correctly, the salad fork is put next to the plate, prongs up and about two and a half inches from the edge of the table. The meat fork is placed at the left of the salad fork. On the extreme left is put the fish fork. As the meat fork is slightly larger than the other forks, its handle descends slightly below its neighbors and its prongs are proportionately high.

The salad knife is put next to the plate on the right. A silver bladed knife is absolutely correct — but if you prefer knifeless salad eating, choose your salad accordingly, and omit the knife. On the right of the salad knife put the dinner knife. (A large knife with a sharp steel blade.) To the right of this goes the fish knife, if it be a fish with bones in it, or skin on it. If the fish chosen is boneless and skinless and easily eaten with fork alone, the knife is omitted. Moreover, since there is a prejudice against more than two knives at each place, it is best to avoid a leaf salad and a fish with bones in the same menu.

This is Correct for Each Place at Formal Lunch Table

The cutting edge of a knife is always turned toward the plate.

The soup spoon is put at the right of the knives, and at the extreme right the oyster fork, or the fruit cocktail spoon. (The oyster fork is the only fork ever put at the right of the plate.)

If the menu is shorter, omit whichever implements are not needed.

GLASSES

Glasses are put above the knives, arranged in whichever order you think is most convenient and looks best.

SALT AND PEPPERS

Salt-cellars and pepper-pots should go between each two plates at table, or individual ones should be placed above each plate.

THE NAPKIN

Correctly, a napkin is laid on each place plate. Should it be necessary to put food on the table before the guests are seated, the napkin is placed at the side of the plate — at the left usually, because two or three forks on the left take up less room than knives, spoons and glasses.

A big dinner napkin, divided into an eight or nine-inch folding, is turned under like a three-fold letter and laid vertically on the plate (or at the left of the forks). Fancy foldings into fans or frogs or other ornate shapes sometimes seen at hotel banquets, are no longer good form in a private house.

SALTED NUT DISHES

Salted nuts are sometimes put in small individual dishes above each place plate. Sometimes they are passed. Often they are omitted altogether.

Certain hostesses always serve them, others never do, just as olives, radishes and celery are served in certain houses, and never in others.

PLACE CARDS

Are fancy place cards in fashion today?

Place cards — elaborate ones — used to be characteristic of the mid-Victorian formal dinner party. But in the present fashion they are perfectly plain cards of heavy bristol board. The rule is that they should not be used for dinners of less than ten persons or for luncheons of less than eight.

Place favors are not fashionable but there is no reason why you should not have them if you like them — especially at Christmas or birthday or other holiday, family or very intimate dinners. On more formal occasions, plain cards are best.

CHAPTER VIII

The Setting of a Formal Lunch Table

The setting of every lunch table—even a formal one—differs from the formal dinner table in details:

1. Table is bare with mats or runners or transparent cloth.
2. There are no candles. (Unless dining room is without daylight.)
3. Bouillon or bisque (if served) is served in cups.
4. Bread and butter plates and butter knives are included.
5. Napkins are smaller in size.

INFORMAL TABLE SETTING

Informal table setting follows the formal pattern as far as the hostess chooses or finds practical.

Cigarettes, matches and ash trays are included in the houses of the moderns but not in those of the conservatives.

Bread and butter plates have been tabu at dinner until lately. But at present they appear regularly on the family dinner table, and often as not at the informal company dinner table as well. The strictly formal dinner table alone refuses to accept them.

The bread and butter plate is put above the forks, and its own knife is laid across it with handle pointing to center of place plate, or parallel with forks. ("Spreader" is a commercial term.)

At lunch or supper, if you serve iced tea or coffee in a tall glass, the long spoon is either put on the table or served on glass plate under the glass.

When coffee or tea is to be served in a cup on a saucer, the spoon should be on the saucer. But the spoon for bouillon or fruit cocktail is placed on the table.

CHAPTER IX

Three Types of Table Service

What are the 3 types of table service?

Accurately speaking, there are three classifications of table service: first, formal or European service — permitting no deviation from ceremonious forms; second, American service — permitting great flexibility; and third, hostess-alone service, which as the term implies, is the most difficult (because it has no rules to go by) as well as the most needful service since it applies to by far the greatest number of American homes. Even so, complete knowledge of formal service is important because every other type of service is derived from the formal pattern.

FORMAL SERVICE

The distinguishing characteristics of formal service are that carving is done by the cook in the kitchen and that the places at table are never left plateless excepting at the end of the course preceding dessert, during the time the table is crumbed. No part of any course is served at table. The only plates that may ever be carried to the table, one in each hand, are for soup and dessert.

To begin with, every place is set with a service plate. When everyone is seated, the first course, whether it be oysters, fruit or soup, is carried from the pantry, two plates at a time — one in each hand and placed on top of the service plate. But if the meal begins with fish or any other hot dish, then the hot plates are carried one at a time, the service plate is removed with one hand and the hot plate substituted with the other, and the dish (equipped with a serving spoon and fork) is held on a folded napkin on the servant's left hand and offered at each person's left. The lady who sits on the right of the host is the guest of honor and is therefore honored by having the untouched dish presented to her first. Of all the existing rules of etiquette — not one is so important at the moment. The hostess who permits herself to be served first before any other woman guest breaks the fundamental law of hospitality, which is courtesy to her guest. If we, the hostesses of America, are going to take first choice for ourselves and give our women guests our leavings, we may as well pitch the entire subject of etiquette into the waste basket. I *mean* it!

THE EXCHANGE PLATE

The formal exaction of an exchange plate is merely this: When a course is served on individual plates, a used plate may never be exchanged for a new plate with food on it. An empty plate must be first exchanged for the used plate and the plate with food on it substituted for the empty plate. Before dessert, all plates are removed as well as salt-cellars and pepper-pots, dishes of salted nuts, unused knives, forks, and butter plates. The table is then crumbed. A dessert plate with a dessert fork and spoon on it, is put at each place. Later this is exchanged for a plate with a finger bowl on it. Or to shorten service, a china plate and on this a glass plate, a spoon and fork and finger bowl is brought on all at once. After dessert has been eaten on the glass plate, this is removed and the china one exchanged or left. Candy—and perhaps fruit— is served last. The serving of cigarettes and cigars is entirely a matter of personal choice and of local custom. In New York the young moderns smoke cigarettes straight through dinner. The average hostess has cigarettes and cigars offered with dessert at really formal dinners, but the old fashioned do not serve cigars and cigarettes at table, until the ladies have left the dining room.

THE HOSTESS "GATHERS EYES"

How does a hostess at dinner let her women guests know that it's time to go back to the living room for coffee?

At all events, when everyone has finished eating, the hostess "gathers eyes" as they used to say. Meaning that she catches the eye of one or two of her women guests and stands. This is the signal for everyone to leave the table. The ladies go back to the living room for coffee. Sometimes the gentlemen go with them or perhaps they have coffee at the dinner table or in the host's study — if he have one! But at an informal dinner they very likely take coffee with the ladies in the living room.

ONE MAID ALONE

When there are perhaps as many as eight to be "waited on" by one maid, she sets a stack of soup plates in front of the hostess and then the soup tureen. Mrs. H. ladles the soup and the maid carries it to each in turn and then goes back to the kitchen. (Water is in each glass and bread and butter on each bread and butter plate when the family sit down.) When she is rung for, the maid takes away the plates, two at a time, stacks them quietly on the serving table behind the screen and then carries out the tureen.

Then she brings in the stack of hot dinner plates and sets them in front of Mrs. H. who puts a piece of meat— also gravy, stuffing or condiment — on the plate at the top of the pile and then, when it is filled, hands it either right or left in the nearest direction toward the person for whom it is intended (in front of whom no formal place plate stands). Meanwhile the maid brings in the vegetables (a double or triple dish is most practical) and proffers this to each person who has been served the meat. She also proffers bread and pours water as necessary. As she returns to the kitchen she carries out the used soup plates. Dessert or salad is served by Mrs. H. and passed by the maid, who then prepares the coffee tray in the living room.

HOSTESS-ALONE

But let us say that you are Mrs. Hostess-Alone, giving a dinner or a luncheon of eight. That seems to me as many as anyone could undertake who is going to attempt to sit at table without having to be a waitress instead of a hostess. The only difference in the setting of your table from that of the formal table pattern is that you put at the places all the implements each person will use — even those for dessert. And you must naturally leave space for whatever dishes of food are to be put on it. Otherwise, you set it with whatever centerpiece you choose. How you set your places depends upon your menu. That, therefore, is the first thing to decide upon.

Since your dinner is in nothing restricted by the requirements of ceremony you are free to choose whichever dishes you can do to perfection and that are practical to serve. Whether they are "party dishes" or not does not matter half so much as that each shall be good of its kind. You know, of course, that selecting a menu practical to serve means avoidance of unnecessary items of preparation or of service. Therefore, don't choose foods that require accompanying sauces or condiments.

Should place plates be used at dinner if the hostess is without a maid?

You can limit your menu to very few dishes, but those few should be substantial — especially for a dinner at which you are expecting men. Instead of the unsatisfying clear soup prescribed for every formal menu, a hostess alone should choose a thick soup. For your main course, let us say you have chicken casserole, which surrounded with vegetables is a complete dish in itself, and then alligator pear salad, with which nothing need be served, and then pie. The advantage of this menu is that you would not have to leave the table at all to serve it.

Unless service plates are to be used for the first course they are merely a handicap, and that fact makes them unsuitable. If this problem were mine, I should put napkins alone at the places and ladle the soup into plates to be put down on the tablecloth — because that would be the simplest thing to do. In front of your husband put the casserole dish on a thick asbestos felt. Or if you have one of the electric bain-maries or buffet containers you could put any other variety of already carved meat in its big compartment and vegetables in the others. Heated dinner plates under a cosey would be put on the serving table next to your husband. The salad prepared on individual plates would stand half on a shelf of your serving table and half on your husband's. Dessert and the stack of dessert plates would stand on the top of your serving table. The further supplies would be on the table, as well as carafes of water and decanters of wine.

When the soup is eaten you take plates on either side of you and then the one next beyond that of the person on your right. How you stack these and remove them to your lowest shelf is something you will have to practice and then make your husband practice since he will have to clear his end of the table exactly as you clear yours. He then serves the meat and vegetables and hands the plates down the table on either side. Places are cleared four by you and four by him. You hand three salad plates right and left and next place beyond your right. You serve dessert and hand the plates down the table on both sides. How you could manage to crumb the table before dessert and to supply finger bowls are problems that you alone must decide. Therefore, it comes to this: Do whatever you find smoothest, simplest and most expedient for YOU!

CHAPTER X

Buffet Dinners, Lunches and Suppers

What is the ideal way to serve dinners, luncheons and suppers if you have no servants?

A buffet, or what is more often called a stand-up supper, or lunch, or dinner, is not only the ideal party for the servantless hostess, but it is one of the very nicest parties possible to give.

A buffet meal, as the name implies, means that the table is set with all sorts of good things to eat. People help themselves, choose where to sit and whom they want to sit next to, and it is all friendly, informal and perfect! It is, moreover, quite as popular among owners of the biggest houses, who have plenty of servants and can give formal dinner parties every day in the year without a thought, as it is for the owner of the littlest house, who has to be cook and waitress as well as hostess. For the latter, it is ideal, since it permits the inviting of twenty or thirty — even more — when a sit-down lunch or dinner at the dining table would be limited to eight, or to as few as six!

INVITATIONS ARE INFORMAL

Since a buffet party is at its best when people know each other well, it is best to choose people in one group, or be sure to ask several from each different group, so that everyone will be likely to find at least a few intimate friends. The invitation is usually written on your visiting card "Stand-up" supper, or "buffet" supper, if you prefer, or lunch, or dinner, whatever it's to be, "Sat. Feb. 25, 7 o'ck." Or the message is telephoned.

ON THE DAY OF THE PARTY

First of all, the chairs are taken out of the dining room and put wherever there is most space. The dining table is set exactly as for a dinner except that you set no places. Candles or candelabra are put at either end of a centerpiece. Then as at a wedding reception or a tea, you set your table with dishes of buttered rolls, sandwiches, salad and cake. You put the coffee service with breakfast cups and cream, as well as small cups, at one end of the table, and a chocolate service or else a bowl of fruit punch with ladle and glasses at the other. Then, leaving room for the hot dishes and plates, you fill the other spaces with piles of cold plates, piles of napkins, rows of forks and rows of spoons — all invitingly arranged. When it is time to serve, stacks of hot plates as well as the dishes of hot foods are put on the table.

THE BUFFET MENU

What dishes should you avoid serving at a buffet supper?
The only difference between dinner or lunch or supper is that dinner usually includes at least two substantial courses of hot food, perhaps one of cream soup, or else a fish pudding or shellfish Newburg, the other as substan-

tial a meat dish as is practical. Every dish must, of course, be chosen so as to be eaten with a fork alone, such as a goulash, a beef and kidney pie, chicken a la king with noodles and mushrooms instead of peppers, or chicken croquettes. A substantial addition to the menu is a big (baking) dish of macaroni or scalloped potatoes, (either white or sweet or corn pudding — something like that). Vegetable salad is typical. (This menu is, of course, merely an indication of dishes that are suitable.) When the main course has been eaten, the platters are taken off and dessert is brought on. The easiest dessert to serve is pie.

A certain hostess, who specializes in buffet suppers and lunches, usually chooses a menu of scrambled eggs and sausages, followed by creamed chicken with wild rice, a vegetable salad, and after that, mixed cut-up fruits. Or else she orders oyster stew and ham mousse with any variety of salad. (Remember that nine men out of ten hate fruit salad "messes.") For dessert, individual dishes of chocolate custard. And to drink, there is cider or fruit cup, chocolate and black coffee — and always plenty of buttered rolls.

BUFFET SERVICE

At buffet meals, how does a hostess direct her guests to serve themselves?

Sometimes the guests sit in the living room and dishes are passed to them. But typically — even in houses which have many servants — the guests file around the dining table, and ladies as well as gentlemen help themselves; or perhaps, as at a dance, the gentlemen fill plates and bring them to the ladies.

When the main hot course and the salad have been eaten, the hot dishes are taken away. In a house without any servants, two members of the family — or intimate friends — stand at either end of the table and serve whatever there may be. Properly a hostess should try to supply plenty of little tables or stands so that one is within easy reach of every chair, to put a glass or cup and saucer on.

WITHOUT LITTLE TABLES

If no little tables can be provided, the guests have to hold their plates on their knees and put their glasses or cups and saucers on the floor beside them. In houses with servants, guests also go to the table and help themselves, if they choose. Otherwise, the servants carry the platters around the room to the guests as they are seated. When there are no little tables and the guests must put their glasses on the floor (there being no other place), it is better to have the iced drink in goblets, which are raised on high stems but substantial, than in low tumblers, which sit flat on the floor, because they are easier to reach. The cup, saucer and spoon necessary for the coffee, tea or chocolate, must be managed as best one can, and in both cases guests must be protectingly conscious of cup or glass, which may otherwise be knocked over.

WHEN GUESTS JUST SIT

I have had a great many letters complaining that the trouble with buffet meals, when there is no servant to pass anything, is that the guests sometimes refuse to help themselves, and "just sit!" The only thing to do then is to say to them, as you would to children at a party, *"Please go into the dining room and get something to eat."* And then if they stand around the table and don't go back into the living room, say "Won't you please go into the living room and sit down?"

CHAPTER XI

ADAPTING THE FORMAL PATTERN TO YOUR NEEDS

In the foregoing pages, I have described the appointments of the table and the correct pattern of dinner service. And now it is important to explain that in giving you the formal rules which assume that the hostess has a cook in the kitchen and a butler or a waitress to do the serving, this does not mean that this information is useless to the hostess who must do her own cooking and dishing as well as serving. On the contrary, she merely applies the pattern exactly as she would do, were she cutting a dress by a pattern that is not her own measure.

THE EVENING OF A DINNER PARTY

And now let us go back to before the arrival of your guests. A few minutes *before* the hour set, you and your husband should be waiting to receive your guests. Your butler or your waitress, or whoever you have engaged to wait on table, should be standing at the front door to open it for each arrival and to take charge of wraps or hats and coats. (If you have no butler or waitress, then your husband must act as substitute.) As each guest enters the room where you are waiting, you go forward, smile, and offer your hand. To everyone at a formal dinner, but otherwise only to someone you know slightly, you say, "How do you do, I am very glad to see you," or "I'm delighted to see you!" — or "I'm so glad you could come." At a dinner of ten or less and to an intimate friend, "How do you do" is contracted to "How do, Mary," "Good evening, Tom" — possibly "Hello, Tom."

IF YOUR GUESTS ARE ALL FRIENDS

They naturally greet each other, sit or stand where they like, and you need do nothing. But if one is a stranger, you must, of course, introduce her — or him — to everyone present at a small party, and to those nearby at a larger one. You say: "Mrs. Stranger, Mrs. Neighbor, Mr. Lake, Mr. Neighbor." As others arrive you say: "Sally, I want you to meet Mrs. Stranger" — then add Sally's name, "Mrs. Nearby."

DINNER IS ANNOUNCED

Whether dinner is announced by a butler, or by a waitress, each merely bows. If you are not looking, he or she says "Dinner is served." Or, if the dining room is next to the living room, the opening of the dining room door serves as an announcement, if whoever you are having in to wait is likely to be awkward in manner.

If the dinner is really formal, the host offers his arm to whoever is the guest of honor, and leads the way to the table and seats her on the right. At a big dinner you have place cards, but at a dinner of eight or less, you go up to whoever is to sit on your husband's right and say, "Shall we go into dinner?" and walk beside her, letting her go into the dining room ahead of you. You seat her by motioning toward a place and say, "Will you sit there on John's right?" You then stand at your own place and tell each person, "Mrs. Jones, you are on John's left. Sally, you are here. Mr. Stranger, next to me" — and so on. Each woman sits at once. The men stand until you have seated the whole table. Then you sit down, and they sit.

WHEN HOSTESS DOES NOT SIT IN HER OWN PLACE

At a dinner of 8, 12 or 16 people, where should the hostess sit?

This is important: At a dinner of eight, twelve or sixteen — any multiple of four — when men and women are of even number, the hostess must give up her seat and sit on the right of the man who is seated opposite the host. This is because it is incorrect to place two women or two men together, unless the number of guests is odd.

HUSBANDS AND WIVES NOT TOGETHER

Is it ever permissible to sit husbands and wives side-by-side at dinner?

It seems unnecessary to add that husbands and wives must never be seated together at a dinner party, but because a number of letters have told me that this archaic custom is not unheard of in the present day, it is well perhaps to include this protest against this provincialism. Conventionally, the guest of honor sits on the host's right, the lady of second rank sits on the host's left. The hostess is seated at the opposite end of the table with the husbands of the two honor ladies on either side of her.

At the end of the meal the hostess stands. This is the signal to leave the table. Only at a formal dinner do the gentlemen give their arms to the ladies and "conduct them to the drawing room" and then leave them. At all other dinners the ladies leave the room and the gentlemen follow and they all drink coffee together—or perhaps the gentlemen stay in the dining room to drink their coffee alone and the ladies alone take theirs in the living room.

CHAPTER XII

THE GREAT AMERICAN RUDENESS IS THAT OF THE HOSTESS WHO SERVES HERSELF FIRST

What is the great American rudeness?

In my opinion — seriously given — I must repeat that there is no excuse for this behavior excepting in a badly equipped house, and in the unusual situation of having one's guest a foreigner to whom forks and spoons are strange and who may not know the use of table implements. In the newest edition of my book "Etiquette," I have given a detailed account of the seven principal origins to which this behavior traces — behavior which in most instances sprang from courteous intention. In the dark ages, for example, when men invited their enemies to dine, so as to poison them, the courteous host (or hostess) tasted the food first as evidence of his innocent intention. Applied to the present day this would still be courteous had a hostess reason to believe someone in her kitchen might put poison in the food, or that it might, by any possible mischance, be spoiled and therefore dangerous. Otherwise, the courteous gesture of protection deteriorates into apparently helping herself to the piece of first choice and then having the second choice piece handed to her guest of honor.

TASTING IS DIFFERENT

In what order should those at table be served wine?

True, when a fine wine is served, it is proper that a little — no more than a sip — be poured into the host's glass, which he tastes to make sure that it is not "corked." If it is, he orders another bottle. And if a hostess might taste a very small portion of food and then if it is not good, order another dish from her kitchen, there would be reason for *her* tasting it. Or if the cook in her kitchen is a very uncertain one, and if by tasting it the hostess can send it back to be cooked a little longer, or to have a forgotten ingredient added, then that too would have a reason of courtesy. And furthermore, if she, let us say, took for the purpose of tasting only so small a fragment as not to disturb the perfect arranging of the dish, this would be quite different from the behavior of the despoiling hostess who breaks into it or gouges a hole out of it so that no one sees its fresh perfection except herself.

But again, if the food is not skillfully dished; if it is sloppily piled on the platter; if there are burnt edges and if by helping herself first the hostess can remove the unsightly pieces and rearrange the whole so as to make it more presentable, then she is right to do so, of course.

IF GUESTS ARE UNSKILLED

Or if, as in the old frontier days, those invited to her table might be unused to the gentler practices of table manners, the courteous hostess would properly put them at ease by helping herself to each dish first, to show them how to use the serving implements and how much to take. And they too might wait until she shows them how to eat with fork or spoon by setting the example. But this behavior, which would be proper under such circumstances, has no place (and never has had) in a perfectly appointed house in which cooking and dishing is expert, and in which the guests are quite as skilled as their hostess in the use of a serving fork and a spoon.

FROM A SERVE-HERSELF-FIRST HOSTESS

In reply to a certain few of my readers who have defended the practice, let me quote first from a letter sent me from one of them:

"I agree, Mrs. Post, there is little need today of examining a cook's dish, since it is seldom that one is so inexpert as to send something into the dining room unfit to eat. And there is less excuse in the house of a hostess who is also her own cook! But I still believe that it is just as courteous to a guest to make the dish easier for her by cutting a helping out of it first. Sometimes an untouched dish can look rather formidable. Can't you see any good in my reasoning that people need not be untutored to feel embarrassed by a dish with no indicated place to break into it or how big a portion to take?"

In answer to this I suggest that if a roast fowl, for example, has been carved and put together again so perfectly as to look untouched, it would be well if the cook who carved it, lifted one slice above the others to show that it may be easily taken out. But under most circumstances nothing is simpler — should we be served first to a really baffling dish — than to say to whoever is waiting at table: "Do I take this?" — prodding lightly with the fork — or, "Do I cut here?" Or if the hostess has reason to suppose her guest of honor may be embarrassed — an old lady perhaps, who does not see very well — then the dish might be cut into as a layer cake is cut into without destroying its form, and the serving spoon inserted beneath the first helping and the fork at hand above it, much in the way a dish is prepared for a child who does not otherwise know what, or how much, to take.

Speaking of children, I wonder — do these same hostesses teach their children that at their own parties they are to take the first helping of ice cream for themselves and to first pick out the piece of cake they themselves like before giving any to their guests?

It is true that the intention which prompts behavior is more important than the behavior itself, but in this particular rudeness, even the motive is unflattering since it supposes that a grown person needs guidance in something that every well trained child of four would resent being supposed not to know.

Obviously, if a hostess is certain that those whom she is expecting have grown accustomed to following after their hostesses, then she would naturally do what she thinks will put them at ease. But, on the other hand, if she is expecting strangers, she should be equally aware of the distressing effect of this behavior upon those not used to it.

In my newspaper column a while ago, I printed a letter from a very distressed Mrs. A. who described her feelings when she lunched alone with a stranger who helped herself to every fresh dish and then had her despoiled leavings proffered to her guest. Mrs. A.'s face grew redder and redder, her mouth dry. She would have preferred, she wrote, had her hostess slapped her face so that she might have left the table and the house instead of having to endure the rudeness of this never before encountered behavior.

In my column I had written that I was sure I would have felt as she did. To this I received a letter from Mrs. X. which is too important not to quote:

Mrs. X. says: "I am not writing to defend the ways of the hostess who has herself served first, nor could I think of following the practice in my own house. However, in many communities such service is accepted, just as other changes in the standards which yesterday exacted, are accepted. It is your right to disapprove of the custom and even an obligation to your readers to give them the benefit of your reasons for your disapproval, but when you seem to sympathize with a guest who permits herself to be as upset as Mrs. A. was, because she read into a deviation from her own way of serving implications of which the hostess never dreamed, so that 'her cheeks flamed, her throat was dry and she couldn't swallow her food,' then surely it is time for that woman to try, if possible, to separate herself from her own emotions, to go off alone and give a thorough check over to her sense of values. So please, dear Mrs. Post, don't put yourself in the class with Mrs. A.; you don't really belong there!"

In answer to this, I am naturally glad not to be considered with Mrs. A. as this reader appraises her. But to be honest, I still think that I would feel very much as she did. I don't think that Mrs. A. was upset by any mere slight to herself. I think it was much more than this. It was a complete repudiation of the meaning of the courtesy which a host (or hostess) must show his guest. The guest must go first, and sit in the best chair, and be served with the best silver and china and linen; above everything, it is the guest who must have the perfectly arranged and untouched dish of honor presented to her.

To the thousands who have for generations been trained (and strictly) to this and all other precepts of courteous behavior, encountering the complete reversal would be like having something one is brought up to honor, destroyed before one's eyes. I remember the letter perfectly and I remember thinking that she must have felt a little as most of us did, I imagine, when we saw newsreel pictures of the burning of the Ikons in Russia. There was an overwhelming emotional shock in witnessing the emblems of the faith of a people being fed to the flames.

By this I mean that if this threatening custom actually spreads into the houses, let us say, that can be looked upon as representative, then certainly courtesy would come to have belittled meaning.

CHAPTER XIII

THE PERFECT HOSTESS

How can a hostess avoid talking about her own worries?
*What is the only time that a hostess may apologize when
something's amiss?*

Tact and kindness are two qualities that every would-be
hostess must possess.

Kindness exacts that she shall think of the effect upon
her guests of what she says and does. Obviously she
should avoid talking about her annoyances or personal
worries, especially those she had in preparing for the
party. Also it would be tactless to say, "I asked everyone
I could think of and you were the only ones who could
come!" The perfect hostess does not become nervous or
over-excited no matter what happens. She has invited
people to her house and hospitality demands that their
sojourn shall be made pleasant. If anything goes so conspicuously wrong that it can't be camouflaged she must
at least make light of it. If the cook leaves just before
her dinner party and no one else can take her place, then
a picnic must be made of the situation as though a picnic
were the most delightful thing possible — which it could
be, very well.

When should a hostess stand to receive her guests at a formal party? At an informal party?

As to mechanical details: At a formal party the hostess stands at the entrance of her living room and receives. At an informal party she hovers near or at least keeps her eye on the door so as to go forward as quickly as possible to greet each newcomer. If she has no one to open the front door for her, she necessarily opens it herself and greets her friends as they enter. By the way, when entering a room, or her house, with a guest, a hostess leads the way only when necessary to hold a door open or to light a light or for other similar reasons. And naturally she asks to be excused for going first.

CHAPTER XIV

On the Subject of Smoking

First of all, let me say frankly and at once, that while there are certain important exactions of courtesy and many questions of taste concerned with every angle of smoking, these details come no nearer to the subject of morality than does drinking black coffee, and no nearer to questionable behavior than powdering one's nose or using a lipstick.

Is it permissible to smoke at dinner when the hostess has not set the table with cigarettes?

On the other hand, since many smokers do make a non-smoker completely miserable, it is for this reason that certain regulations of courtesy are expected to be observed. One who sits at the table of a hostess who does not set her table with cigarettes, should not smoke. Nor may one ever smoke in the house of one who offers no cigarettes, without making doubly sure that the hostess has no objections. To ask, "Do you mind if I smoke?" — which is the plainest requirement of courtesy — is not quite enough. One must be sure that consent is given willingly.

saying "no" to alcohol

Are you at a loss to know how to refuse a cocktail?

It is never necessary to drink a beverage with alcohol in it if you do not care to. It is just as easy to say, "No thank you," to a cocktail as to a dish at table which you happen not to care for or to which you are allergic. In the first place, at every cocktail party there should always be at least one kind of non-alcoholic drink, such as tomato juice or ginger ale or else half pint bottles of milk with straws to drink the milk through, for those who do not like the stronger drinks.

It is inexcusably bad manners to let a guest remain thirsty because no non-alcoholic beverage is proffered.

CHAPTER XV

To Those Who Worry About Party Giving

Does party giving make you worried and upset?

It seems to me — I don't know why I haven't thought of it before — that the letters sent me by worried hostesses and perplexed guests would shrink to a fraction of their daily number, if only the words "hostess" and "guest," "entertain" and "formal" might be put away and forgotten until an exceptional occasion of ceremony made it necessary to get them out.

Of course, if you are in the Diplomatic Service or if you hold official position in Washington, then plainly you will be expected to play the formal role of host, hostess, or guest, almost every day and evening in the week. But if you are one of the average, home-loving and at-home staying majority, the chances are small that you will think of "expecting guests for dinner," or "guests to play bridge," or "guests coming to spend a week!" It is far more likely that the thought in your mind will be that "John and Mary, Joe and Jane are coming to dinner," or "Quite a lot of people (all thought of by first name) are coming in for tea and cocktails, or for stand-up supper." But certainly the word which comes into the mind of most of us when we think of our relatives and intimate friends, is not "guests." Surely it would seem strange to think of Aunt Susie as a house guest, to whom we are to be hostess! And yet, this is just the point of view that many people take.

Therefore, let us first of all stop thinking of ourselves as masquerading in a role not even recognizable to our every day mirrors, receiving a number of strange figures masquerading as guests, and let us try, if we can, to realize that a hundred Johns and Marys are Johns and Marys still — and then perhaps we will overcome the only handicap there is to party giving. After all, we know very well that real success in party giving is not half so often due to the possession of unlimited money, as it is to the possession of a happily hospitable point of view.

WATCH OUT FOR HOSTESS FRIGHT

What's the best way to stop "hostess fright"?
What are the 3 ingredients of successful party giving?

Requirement Number One, therefore, is to watch out for symptoms of hostess fright! The moment you find yourself thinking, "Oh, I know it'll be a failure! — nobody will have a good time — I'm sure they're only coming because they didn't know how to say 'no' — I'm sure the food isn't good enough!" Stop such thoughts at once! The best way to stop them is to put yourself in the opposite place. If you were going to dine with John and Mary or to spend the evening with Joe and Jane, would you be as critical of their talents, or equipment, as you are imagining them to be of yours? Of course, if it is possible that you hate all parties, no matter where they are given or by whom; that you don't really like people enough to even see very much of those you consider your friends, then perhaps neither party giving nor party going is for you, and there is little sense in reading any more of this. But, if you do like people and if your husband likes them, and you would be eager to give parties, if only you could give them without worrying yourself sick, then the rest of this article may perhaps have in it something of use to you.

Requirement Number Two is of greatest importance: It is to take pains in your selection of people. Either ask those who belong in the same small group, or those who are likely to have interests or tastes in common.

Requirement Number Three is food. This, while important, is not necessarily the beginning and end of entertaining. In other words, food can play a major part — and in certain houses it does. But in other houses the part it plays is comparatively small. And it is possible, when company is its specialty — that we go to this last house with even more pleasure than to the first. After all, if we are going where we know provisions are likely to be meagre, we *can* prepare for this deficiency by fortifying ourselves with a slice of bread and butter, and a cup of bouillon or coffee before leaving home, but there is no way to fortify ourselves against an evening with dull company.

Ideally, your friends should be able to count on you for good company and good food both! The point to be made therefore, is to invite people because *you* think they are interesting, or amusing, or divertingly ornamental. Or, perhaps for no reason that you can put your finger on, except you just *like* them, and you feel sure that others will like them too.

IF SHE LOVES HIM SURELY WE CAN LIKE HIM

Do you know how to change David Dull into David Delighting?

How can you overcome the problem of making dull husbands of your friends acceptable to your other guests?

It is true that there are always an ineffectual few who have to be asked because they are married to the women or the men you like best. But again I think the only way to meet this handicap is not to worry about it. Don't wring your hands and say, "What shall we do about George Grump and David Dull?" After all, Diana finds George admirable and Gloria adores David! So *why* believe that to everyone they seem as irritating or stupid as they do to you? And perhaps if you would sing praises of their good points (they must have some or Diana and Gloria wouldn't have married them) you would certainly find them less of a liability than if you go around apologizing: "I know I gave you a terrible place at table — George Grump is enough to ruin the evening for anyone!" Or, "Lucy dear, I had to put you next to that deadly David, but I'll do something for *you* some time!" How much better to say, "You know, if one is clever enough to make him talk, George Grump has a brilliant mind!" Or, "David is such a darling!" In short, to apologize for your guests is just about the greatest mistake possible to make. Apologies for anything should never be made except under circumstances of unavoidable accident, impossible to hide. Even so, make the apology casual: "I hope you *like* cold canned food! If the electricity comes on we might sometime have dinner!" Otherwise, the one important consideration of food is that it shall be *good* of its kind.

IMPORTANT TO HAVE FOOD OF RIGHT TEMPERATURE

How important is the temperature of food?

The really important point is one which a surprising number of good cooks completely overlook! This is the obvious fact that good food is dependent upon the requirements of temperature. Hot food must be so hot that even a salamander should have to eat around the outer edges inward in order not to blister his tongue. Cold food, on the other hand, must be *cold.*

AFTER DINNER

Do you know that most fascinating of after-dinner games — The Game?

To the hostess who worries about what to do after dinner when those invited don't all play bridge — or what to do if she gives a large but very simple evening at home, the answer is game-playing which is the rage of the hour; so why not join all the other enthusiasts who are playing "The Game," or go back to Charades or Clumps, or anything you may choose or revise and call *"Your* Game."

"The Game," in case you don't know it, is evidently a descendant of both Twenty Questions and Charades. As well as I can describe it in a few words it is played this way:

A referee, two teams, and a captain for each team are chosen. The referee goes off by himself and writes a list of ten names of books, or names of plays, or movies, or songs, or short familiar quotations, or advertising slogans. Each team goes into a room by itself. The referee takes his place at a point equally distant from each. The two captains go to the referee and are told the first sentence or word on his list. The two captains shut themselves in with their teams and a spy from the opposing team. "The

Game" is to guess the word, somewhat as the word in Twenty Questions is guessed. The captain must act the word and can only answer by nodding yes or no. The spy in each camp watches to see that the captain does not spell out the word or speak.

As soon as a member of the team thinks he has guessed the answer, he rushes to whisper it to the referee. If he is wrong, the referee shakes his head and the mis-guesser goes back and tries again. If he is right, then he wins that point for his team, and becomes its captain. The referee gives him a credit mark and the name of the next subject. After telling his team what the answer was, he assumes the role of dumb actor. The team which guesses all ten titles first wins.

CHAPTER XVI

WHAT TO WEAR AND WHEN

To begin with, let me answer a letter which takes me to task for taking the correctness of dress seriously. Quote: "What difference can it make to anyone else whether Mary Blank wears a long dress or a short one, or a thick one or a thin one, a hat or none? Surely, she is not offending anyone else, nor hurting their feelings, nor is she failing to contribute to beauty by wearing what is in her opinion, becoming and comfortable. Quoting a maxim of your own: 'Comfort is another word for beauty' — so what more can be said?"

To this I must reply that comfort — meaning ideal suitability to use — is another word for beauty, but unsuitability either to use or to situation is always an offense to beauty. As I have written in chapter two of this booklet, a comfortable arm chair, inviting to sit in, does give a homelike quality (which is beauty) to a living room. On the other hand, yellow shoes and a khaki flannel shirt with a man's tail coat — no matter how much more comfortable they would be than new patent leather pumps and a stiff white shirt and collar — would not only make the man himself an object of derision, but his outlandish appearance would mar the effect of the general assembly in which he finds himself — exactly as a blotted word in a letter not only mars that one word but spoils the effect of the whole page. More than that, clothes not only affect our appearance, they ARE our appearance, and the subject of dress is irrational only when carried to extremes — either as an obsession or as an antipathy. One extreme is as unreasonable as the other. But that we shall on all occasions be conventionally dressed is quite as important as that we shall have good manners and speak good English. A few requirements of convention follow:

ON A CITY STREET

Should a woman ever appear on the street wearing a hat but no gloves?
What are the smartest type clothes for street wear?

Always wear a hat and gloves. If you wear a long coat, be sure that your dress is not hanging in uneven points below. For street wear, tailored clothes are smartest. Conspicuous clothes that attract attention should be avoided.

IN A SMART RESTAURANT IN THE DAY TIME

When should you remove your gloves on entering a restaurant?
Should a woman remove her hat in a restaurant?

Wear the same clothes as on the street. A smart tailored suit with a good looking blouse and becoming hat is considered quite as proper for a woman of leisure as for a business woman even at a lunch party, and especially one given in a hotel or club. But top of dress or blouse (covered by coat on street) can be as light or bright in color as you please. Take off gloves as soon as you are seated at table, but do not take off hat, and do NOT comb your hair at table!

IN RESTAURANT, EVENING

Is it ever permissible to wear a hat with an evening dress?

In a very smart restaurant wear an evening dress not too conspicuously cut. If you wear a hat with a low cut dress it must be only a distinctly evening variety — with a hat always wear gloves. If the man with whom you are dining is not wearing a dinner coat, then you should not wear an evening dress. However, a dress just off the floor with a high cut back or else a cape or a matching coat would be suitable. However, if the man is in tweeds, then you ought to wear strictly day clothes and a hat.

IN DINING ROOM OF HOTEL IN WHICH YOU ARE STAYING

Although a hat is always correct with street clothes, you can perfectly well go into the dining room without a hat — particularly for breakfast. It is only in a restaurant to which people come in from outside to lunch or dine that a hat should be worn in the day time, and evening dress at night.

SHALL I WEAR A HAT?

What is the rule for deciding whether or not you should wear a hat in any situation?
Is it permissible for a hostess to wear a hat at a luncheon at her own home?

When in doubt a safe rule is to ask yourself about the dress you are wearing. "Could I wear it in the day time?" If the answer is "no" then you should not wear a hat. If the answer is "yes, but not on the street," then wear a small brimless type that is suitable for evening. If you are wearing street or sports clothes, then a hat is obligatory. Fashionable women always wear hats in the day time or even late afternoon in houses not their own. In fact, many fashionable hostesses wear hats at lunch in their own houses but they do not wear hats at tea or cocktail parties at home. But if it is customary in your own community not to wear a hat at table in a private house, then it is best to do what others do.

GLOVES

Should a lady ever remove her gloves when shaking hands?
Should you apologize for your gloves when shaking hands?

Always wear gloves on the street. A really smart woman wears them always — even in the country. Always wear gloves in a restaurant, in a theatre, when you go to lunch, or to a formal dinner, or to a dance. Always take them off when you eat. A lady NEVER takes off her gloves to shake hands, no matter when or where, and NEVER apologizes for wearing gloves when shaking hands. The only exception is when she is wearing earth-stained gardening gloves, which might seem marring to the hand or the fresh glove of another. She would pull it off, or say "I can't shake hands." Few people wear long gloves except when sitting in a box at the opera or at a very formal dinner (meaning one of ceremony). However, the question of length is one of transient fashion.

BUSINESS CLOTHES

The unfailing directions for clothes worn in an office are tailor-made, smart to the last degree and in perfect taste but in nothing conspicuous. Neat, beautifully done hair, and no little girl effect of hair flowing loose upon shoulders. In hot weather, very short sleeves are permissible, but NOT cut-out arm holes or low back or too transparent materials. Deep mourning clothes are not suitable in an office, but you can wear black and white or gray. Also it is not unusual for women to wear mourning bands on tailored coats, but not on dresses.

IN THE COUNTRY

Where is it proper to wear slacks? To wear shorts?

In the country, as everywhere else, very young women wear on the country club veranda, or at a lunch, every variety of simple one-piece dresses or sports clothes. Hats and gloves optional except at church and other especial occasions. Slacks proper on a boat or on the beach or at picnics. Shorts proper (for the young and slim) on tennis courts and for occasions when utility gives them an excuse. Women not so young — especially those inclined to rotundness — should avoid both, except in the wilds. On a beach, very abbreviated bathing dresses and even bare-toed sandals are possible on the young and pretty, but even so "swimming skin tights" should observe a few decencies. That older women should wear enough covering to be becoming, is obvious.

Is it ever permissible to wear bare-toed sandals with an evening dress?

Bare-toed sandals with evening dresses are too revolting to mention. Otherwise, there are no directions for evening clothes except that the simpler, the prettier.

There is nothing more beautiful than a very young girl or boy dressed principally in sun-tan, but I do think that the reason for undress which is unhampered freedom in swimming, would not be lost even if bathing trunks had an inch or two added to their length.

MEN AS WELL AS WOMEN AT WEDDINGS

At a morning or early afternoon wedding in the city followed by a breakfast, women wear becoming street clothes suitable in the season of the year, or in the country they would wear the same clothes that they would wear to church. In town men would wear cutaway coats and striped trousers exactly as at an afternoon wedding. In the country they would wear gray or tan or white flannel trousers and gray or brown or blue sack coats.

At a late afternoon wedding followed by a reception of any importance women wear afternoon dresses either of street length or longer. (Suitable hats and gloves are, of course, always worn with day clothes.)

The hardest question to decide is what to wear at a half past five o'clock wedding that is to be followed by a reception. Such an invitation should include "afternoon dress" or "evening dress" in small letters in the lower left corner for the especial benefit of the men who otherwise have no idea whether in broad daylight they should wear tails and be right later on, or wear cutaways and be right at the ceremony. The problem of this between day and night hour is simple enough for a woman in this present day fashion of an evening dress that is turned into a day dress by wearing a jacket and a hat that later can be taken off. But a man can't turn day clothes into evening ones by any means as yet invented. (Perhaps this may give the tailors something to think about.) Quite seriously then, the only thing for a man to do is to agree with several others to go in day clothes or evening ones, which would at least assure him of finding these several others in clothes like his own!

Guests who are not going on to the reception need not dress as much as they otherwise would.

A public dinner invitation which advises "Dress Optional" is always puzzling for a man to decide whether he has the choice of tails or dinner coat or whether the choice is between a dinner coat and a business suit. The answer to this is that if he wears a dinner coat he can't be wrong!

CHAPTER XVII

Rules of Escape For Host or Hostess

Since many rules of etiquette which were established in days when the world of fashion lived in big houses run by many servants, are utterly impractical in this present day of small houses run by one maid or by none at all, it is obvious that newer and more useful rules must be devised to take the place of those which have in certain cases become useless. Among the situations particularly needing new rulings are those which have heretofore exacted the helplessness of the host and hostess, whenever visitors have been admitted under their roof. Although many of these newly devised rules would not be necessary were more thoughtfulness shown by the visitors, there are other situations in which the visitors have no way of knowing that their visit is inopportune unless the host or hostess in one way or another tells them so.

THOUGHTLESS VISITORS

What should a woman do when her guests stay into the family meal time and she has nothing extra in the house to serve?

In the class of thoughtless visitors belong those who arrive before a meal hour and stay and stay until the hour is long past. For example, when the Towns who go to the country cottage of the Greens and carelessly (and still worse, intentionally) stay past meal time, they should have no right to think it unfriendly on the part of Mrs. Green if she says frankly, "I do wish we could ask you to stay to dinner" (or supper, or whatever the meal) "but there isn't an extra thing in the house!" The answer to this is "Oh, I AM sorry. I had no idea it was so late!" and take leave immediately. The utterly unforgivable answer would be, "Oh, we don't mind what we have — just a cup of tea and a piece of bread will do perfectly." The only reply to this is a bolted door against these intruders forever after!

If you pay a social visit and have reason to suspect that your hostess was planning to go out, what should you do?

Another thoughtless example is that of the visitor who fails to notice that the hostess is either dressed for the street, or else in an apron which quite plainly shows that she is busy with her housework. In such cases the visitor should ask, "Were you just going out" — or "Have I come at a moment when you are very busy? Please don't let me interfere. I will come some other day." To either of these situations, the hostess should answer the truth. "Well, I do have to go to school for Mollie," or "I am meeting Mother at the station," or "I was in the middle of baking," or "I was just getting ready to bathe the baby," whereupon the visitor quickly departs and returns at another hour of another day.

YESTERDAY THE HOSTESS WAS TRAPPED

What should a housewife do when someone calls unexpectedly and she has duties or an engagement elsewhere?

According to the etiquette of yesterday the hostess had to make believe that she had nothing to do but sit down and talk to a visitor, all the time worrying about something undone or glancing at the clock, approaching an engagement elsewhere or feeling that her clothes were not only unsuited to the "parlor" but probably untidy. Meanwhile, conversation was certainly disconnected and footless. And yet all she had to say was, "Oh, please come to see me when I shall be free to enjoy your visit, won't you?"

What should you do when guests come to visit you in the city and expect you to accompany them to amusements you feel you cannot afford?

Or again, when the Out-of-Towns who are really dear friends of the Cityclerks, are invited to spend a week with them, write in their letter of acceptance that they are looking forward to their delightful glimpse of city life— going to the opera, to such and such plays, and also to the night clubs, Mrs. Cityclerk who has never been in a night club and sits in the third balcony at the opera about once a year, should certainly write to tell her visitors that she wants them to feel completely free to go to all the places they want to, in other words, to treat their apartment as though it were a hotel.

HELPLESS HUSBAND

What should you do when friends who come to play bridge seem willing to play very late when your family has to be up early next morning?

Another situation is when guests who come in for the evening to play bridge insist upon playing rubber after rubber until the host who gets up early in the morning gets more and more tired and nervous, perhaps because he has a very important appointment next day. His wife should in this case come to his rescue and say, "I'd love to play another rubber or as many as you like, but Harry had a headache when he came home and he really must go to bed! We could play three-handed if you like."

How can a wife help her husband escape from late-staying guests?

What determines the real difference between the courtesy of tact and the discourtesy of brutal frankness?

When visitors are women, the husband might very well manage to escape to his own room, but when a man has come to see him, his wife is helpless unless she plays the part of a trained nurse and says, "Jim, you know the doctor says you must get eight hours sleep after that flu attack you had!" On the other hand, if Jim is a strappingly strong man then he will just have to go without many hours of sleep as best he can.

It is, I agree, very hard to find a way to protect those who don't like evening visitors from those who are differently inclined. But in mid-week when a man (and probably his wife too) must get up early next morning, it is best in the end if they say to everyone frankly that they never sit up late except on Saturday night. In other words, it is best in the end to be frank in the beginning.

One last word: In all situations where frankness is the essential solution, it is well to remember that courtesy is really much more a question of the brusqueness or the kindliness of manner in which an explanation is made.

CHAPTER XVIII

Art Is Really Heart in Hospitality

Is it necessary to spend lots of money to give successful parties?

It is doubtful if any other remarks are made to me so often as those which take it for granted that fairly lavish money-spending is the one unavoidable requirement for party giving. In short, it is plain that the majority of people firmly believe that the only really successful hostess is she who lives in the biggest house, equipped with the largest staff of servants, and who need not worry about paying the butcher, the grocer, the baker, and so on. When, in fact, believing that hospitality at frugal expense is not good enough to be worth attempting, is very much like believing that the salaries paid to motion picture actors alone guarantee a play worth going to see.

Obviously, if a hostess and host have certain definite and essential talents, in addition to the money to provide every material detail, the result is complete perfection. But between accepting an invitation to the Richan Crudes or to the John Welcomes, there is not much doubt about who amongst us would accept which. The actual counterparts of John and Mary Welcome always come into mind at the mere mention of the phrase "successful party giving." And this story is the true one of a bride and groom who went as strangers with the slimmest purses, to live in Philadelphia.

It is true they had definite advantages: His father was at that time Governor and had many friends, who in turn wrote to friends of their own in Philadelphia who saw to it that John and Mary were invited to all of the general Balls and parties. This may sound like complete success! But the reverse side of the picture is that they did not even know by sight a single one of those whose names were engraved at the tops of the invitations. Moreover, John's earnings were enough for necessities but very inadequate for any extras. And their clothes were as few as his dollars.

Their one room apartment, flattered by being called a "studio" was at the top of three walk-up flights of stairs. Many a bride, looking at the sheaf of invitations from the most prominent hostesses in town, would have been torn by conflicting emotions. On the one hand she would have been pleased to be asked, but unable to imagine going to all these smart houses evening after evening in the same clothes. Furthermore, she would never have imagined it possible to return a single invitation. The average bride would have exclaimed: "Oh, John. We can't go, possibly!"

But not Mary. She saw to it that her husband's few evening shirts and waistcoats were kept laundered and that his and her own clothes were neat and pressed. And the fact that she wore the same two dresses alternately, and that she and John had to walk to every party — no matter what the weather — didn't bother either of them for a minute.

How does one repay her obligations when she has been invited to the houses of people of great wealth?

It is a Cinderella story, of course, of charm and personality triumphing over the material handicaps of a slim purse. He told me, not long ago about the plans they made for the first party they ever gave. Her list of guests to be experimented upon, included several patronesses of the Assembly Balls and two or three governors of the most conservative clubs.

"Oh, John, it is too good to believe," said she, "that we will have all these lovely people here at last under our own roof with us." The engraved names no longer belonged to unknown people.

"I don't know," said he doubtfully, "how Mrs. Elderly and Colonel Ruff Ridah can walk up all our stairs!"

"We'll borrow chairs," announced she, "from our landlord, and put them on the landings so that those who mind the stairs very much can rest."

"But what can we have for supper?" asked he.

"That's easy," she answered. "We'll have corned beef hash with plenty of potato and we'll have bread and butter and tea."

Luckily their wedding presents had included plenty of silver and china. The tea set was polished to mirror brightness and set at one end, and a chafing dish at the other, on a table at one side of the studio room. And there was plenty of bread and butter — with the crust left on because Mary thought it would go further and also she couldn't bring herself to wastefully throw the crust away. They also had mottoes, made of strips of quotations wrapped around clear candy enclosed in fringed paper. As it turned out they had to hire camp chairs, not only for the landings, but to provide seats for their guests.

The studio was made gay with its print curtains and

slip covers (made by Mary, of course) and bright by many lighted candles which they stuck on red painted boxes of different heights. Also there were pots of pink geraniums on the window sills. The studio was gay, the hosts so friendly, and the party such a success, that before long few invitations were more sought after than Mary's and John's. In trying to find a reason for the real charm of their parties, I can think of nothing except that they themselves had a joyous "kindling" quality that seemed to make everyone bright and sparkling, just as kindling turns gray logs into a warming fire.

Wherein lies the knack of making people enjoy one another's company?

They were both so genuinely glad you had come, and they had a knack of making their own gladness in some way contagious. I remember one evening when a certain brilliant man who was also a gourmet, found himself placed next to one whom he considered the stupidest woman in town. Mary passed by, noticed his eye on the clock, and said, "If you want the best receipt in the world of Chinese Curry or Cafe Brullot, perhaps YOU can persuade Mrs. Brown to give them to you, though," she added, with a twinkle in her eye, "she has kept them a secret from everyone else!" If it hadn't been for this quick-witted perception of Mary's, these two might never have found a subject of conversation congenial to both, and Mary's party might have gone down in their memories as a very deadly evening.

This knack for finding ground in common between people of alien interests, is by no means as easy as it may sound to follow. Most people who attempt it over-do it and sound like the barkers of side shows at a County Fair. John, on the other hand, had talent for rearranging people if they didn't look particularly happy. He could, for instance, adroitly unloose Mr. Snobley from the side of Mrs. Tuppence by fortuitously walking up with Mr. Highborn, who he suspected would find her the most charming woman in the room. Whereupon that left Mr. Snobley free to be taken in the direction of a Mrs. Minta Gold.

Throughout the years of the great inflation, what one *had* seemed to most people to count much more than what one *was*, but not so to John and Mary. It is true, they prospered too, and moved into a big house and gave formal dinners which began in the drawing room with caviar and progressed through terrapin and canvasbacks to a brandy of Napoleon served to the gentlemen in the smoking room at the end of dinner, in big soap bubble glasses. Today their parties are midway between, but their popularity has never changed. Whether the food they proffered was bread (with the crust left on) and butter and tea, or whether it might be caviar, canvasback, does not matter a bit. It is they themselves, and their warm appreciative friendliness which draws people to wherever they live.

What is the ideal way to select people for a party?
Can a hostess develop the art of selecting guests so that harmony and successful party giving result?

The gift for people is much the same as the gift for arranging flowers. In each case it is a matter of arranging them in such a way as to present them at their best. There is all the difference between liking to select people as the buyer for a shop selects goods to sell to the public, and choosing a group for this party or that one because you know that they will be agreeable to one another. The unsuccessful hostess gathers a lot of people exactly as they happen to come: sunflower next to violet, orchid next to goldenrod, bougainvillea next to scarlet sage, with the result that each is displayed at its unbecoming worst. Whereas the ideal method of making a party list is to choose your guests exactly as an artist combines flowers in a bouquet; the greater the artist, the greater the variety he can combine, of course.

Having made sure in this way that your bouquet of guests is in harmony, you need not really worry about any of the less important details. Dozens of them can go wrong and few people will notice, and fewer still will care.

CHAPTER XIX

WHAT VALUE ETIQUETTE?

And now at last it is perhaps quite unnecessary to explain to the readers of this little book that the subject of etiquette is not only unlimited in scope, but it is an essential one to every person in every civilized community. And yet no word in our language is so greatly misunderstood, so falsely interpreted as this word etiquette. Many people who have never stopped to consider whether their way of doing things is a best way, a not very good way, or a quite wrong way, are likely to think of the whole subject as an over-fussy collection of finicking rules intended for social up-starts, but of no earthly use to everyday people who lead everyday lives. To other people who are self-conscious about their manners, uncertain about their ways of doing things, the very word etiquette suggests a sort of quiz made up of trick questions that have no purpose further than to exalt those who know the answers and to humiliate those who do not. Actually its so-called rules and directions are exactly like those for cooking which have through long usage been proved to give best results.

When I wrote the first edition of my "Blue Book," I wrote it exactly as if it had been a cook book. As little fuss and trimming as possible, and as many exactly-what-you-do-next-facts. You will notice this same method has been carried out in this little green book as in the big blue one. A few details — those for example which describe the setting of a formal dinner or lunch table, the essential list of silver, the details of correct service — are unchangeable details taken, therefore, from one or two chapters in my book, "Etiquette."

As a matter of fact, the subject of etiquette in its larger aspect is a record of every situation in life: it is a record of the ways and means that people most familiar with each of these contacts and experiences have found practical — that is all it is. Every detail, no matter how trifling it may seem, is important if it contributes to pleasantness, to beauty, to comfort, or to taste. If it contributes none of these things then it need be given no consideration. The rules of etiquette are the rules of civilized living. Everything we do, everything we say, everything we choose, every impulse we check or obey is governed by a precept of taste, of experience, of kindness, of worldly knowledge, of ethics — in short, etiquette.